I'm Living the Life I Want!

Get Paid while Pursuing Your Pasion

By: Ruth Thompson

9781635014235

I0510834

Publishers Notes

Disclaimer – Speedy Publishing LLC

This publication is intended to provide helpful and informative material. It is not intended to diagnose, treat, cure, or prevent any health problem or condition, nor is intended to replace the advice of a physician. No action should be taken solely on the contents of this book. Always consult your physician or qualified health-care professional on any matters regarding your health and before adopting any suggestions in this book or drawing inferences from it.

The author and publisher specifically disclaim all responsibility for any liability, loss or risk, personal or otherwise, which is incurred as a consequence, directly or indirectly, from the use or application of any contents of this book.

Any and all product names referenced within this book are the trademarks of their respective owners. None of these owners have sponsored, authorized, endorsed, or approved this book.

Always read all information provided by the manufacturers' product labels before using their products. The author and publisher are not responsible for claims made by manufacturers.

This book was originally printed before 2014. This is an adapted reprint by Speedy Publishing LLC with newly updated content designed to help readers with much more accurate and timely information and data.

Speedy Publishing LLC

40 E Main Street, Newark, Delaware, 19711

Contact Us: 1-888-248-4521

Website: http://www.speedypublishing.co

REPRINTED Paperback Edition: 9781635014235:

Manufactured in the United States of America

DEDICATION

To my twin sister, Rita - you have always been there whenever I needed you. Thank you.

TABLE OF CONTENTS

Chapter 1- Your Passion as Solution to Debt

Everyone has a passion. It often manifests during childhood and is pursued through play or it is stumbled upon as we age but almost immediate put aside for more practical things like work and building a family. Children are free to actively pursue the things that interest them, but as they age they are encouraged to go after more practical pursuits often putting their passion aside. However, it isn't impossible or impractical to continue to follow your passion even as you age. Doing what you love even as a hobby can go a long way to living a life that you enjoy. There was a time when people weren't encouraged to follow or even consider passion when living their lives. Survival was the most important and that often meant working from sun up to sundown with only room for sleeping and eating. Things like hobbies and passion weren't discussed or even considered because there was no room for it.

Thanks to societal changes like the Industrial Revolution and the advent of technology, we no longer have to toil so hard just to survive. We have the luxury of only having to work 40 hours a week (give or take) and having weekends off to do things like goof off, go on vacation or discover and pursue our passion. With our overly scheduled lives that might not seem like much time but any time spent actively seeking your heart's desire is better than no time at all.

Over time, we often forget the passions of our childhood or even the ones we discover as we age. So discovering our passion is often the first step down a path of actively pursuing it. If you're unsure how to go about discovering your passion, here are some steps to get you thinking in the right direction.

1. Take a stroll down memory lane and make a list.

Think back to when you were a kid. What are some of the things you really loved doing? What are some of the things you thought were really cool but couldn't do? What are some of the things you really wanted to try but didn't think you'd be good at it? Write everything down, no matter how silly it may sound. This is a great time to throw practicality completely out of the window and live in a fantasy land, even if only for a moment. Take some time with this but not too long. You don't want to spend the rest of your days dreaming about what your passion could be. You want to actually pursue it!

2.Consider your current job.

What are some things that you are tasked with doing at work that you enjoy? While this may not be as fun as strolling down memory lane, it's important to consider what you enjoy doing as an adult. Make a separate list. It may be best to do this while you're actually at work so you can fully assess your daily tasks. Write down everything that comes to mind even the most mundane tasks. While it may not seem very cool to write that you enjoy creating spreadsheets or collating papers, it still counts. Passion isn't always considered cool or trendy but if you love it, you should explore it.

3. What would you do if you had all of the money you needed and didn't have to worry about paying your bills?

We all have to work to live. Yes we no longer have to work from sun up to sun down just to put food on the table (for the most part), but we still have bills to pay and mouths to feed (even if it's just your own mouth). This is another fun exercise and you're allowed to be as fanciful as you like. Practicality has no place in the world where all of our financial responsibilities are met and we're able to just live as we please.

Make a separate list. Now that you have these three lists, review them. You may notice some similarities between the lists. Take note of the similarities. If you're a fan of color coding, you can color code them or you can just make a separate list. The similarities you discover will lead you down the road to pursuing your passion. In fact, you may find some passions that are ripe for you to begin exploring right away. However, don't throw away the other lists. Keep them in a safe place that you can easily access. Some of the other things on your list may be worth exploring at a later date. Even if it's an interest on one list, it could still take you down a path to your passion.

I'm Living the Life I Want!

The cool thing about passions is that they can often lead to other things you really enjoy. The next step in this process is to go out and do some of the things from your final list. Approach this process in an exploratory manner, don't rush it. Finding your passion shouldn't be approached like a timed task. The whole point is to discover things that you enjoy and then do them. I realize that may be easier said than done but it's an important step in the process.

So now that you have a list of some things you'd like to explore, you may be unsure how to proceed. Here are some tips on how to dig further into your newfound passion journey.

1.Take a class.

There are tons of classes, both online and offline on almost any topic around. Do a quick web search for your topic and "class" to see what types of classes are available. For example, if one thing you wanted to do as a kid was climb trees and you live in Boston, do a web search of "climb trees class" or "climb trees class Boston" and you will begin to find classes, courses and articles about climbing trees and the ones specific to the Boston area.

2.Join a group

There are wonderful websites where people are encouraged to create groups around a specific interest. I encourage everyone to create a profile on these sites. They're usually free to join and are great resources. Once you create a profile, you can do a search for any interest and the site will show you all of the groups related to that interest in your area. Then you can join the groups and participate in their discussion. The different groups are free to join for the most part. The ones that require a fee are typically very affordable and may be worth the extra investment. It's a great way to not only explore your interests but meet other people who share your interests and possibly make new friends.

3. Read a book

If you're not feeling particularly adventurous at the moment but still want to dive into these interests you forgot you had, reading is a great way to explore it without leaving your house. While I do encourage you to eventually get out into the world and actually explore your interests through action, reading is a good step. You can do a search of your favorite online book seller, visit your local bookstore or spend some time in your local library. Get as many books as you can read at one time and spend some time between those pages exploring your interests.

Correcting the Society's Take on a Making Money from Passion

Congratulations! You've started down the path of finding your passion. By now you should have at least identified a few things that you are passionate about and be exploring at least one or two of them. Hopefully, you're enjoying this foray into fun and learning more about yourself. In the meantime, let's get back to why you stopped pursuing your passions in the first place; practicality.

Many of the things we're passionate about aren't really the most practical things to do when you grow up and become a "responsible" adult (Let's be honest. Who actually feels like a responsible adult when you become one?). Once you've settled into "real life" and started working and taking care of all of the not so fun adult responsibilities, you may find it challenging to do things that don't contribute to your personal bottom line. It may feel indulgent to take time off to do things like fly kites or write short stories when they don't directly contribute to maintaining your household. So while you may do them occasionally, they will often be put off when more pressing "responsible" concerns arise like having to take the car in for repairs or take the kids to their extracurricular activities.

While doing something purely for enjoyment may feel indulgent, most passion pursuits require a level of skill. Some people really enjoy building websites and that's obviously a marketable skill but if your passion is more obscure, it may be tough to find the practical skills behind it. Don't give up and move on to something that you kind of like and abandon your passion, though. It is possible to find the practical skills behind your passion. I'm going to take two examples of passions, one more common and the other more fanciful and show you how it can be done.

Writing Short Stories

Let' start with the more common one. There are many secret writers out there who love to create poetry or prose be it non-fiction or fiction but we all know that most authors don't end up on the best seller list. In fact, most writers never make a dime from their writings. But just because they may not profit from their narrative musings, it doesn't mean that writers aren't building a skill set. While it may seem obvious, there are some skills there that might not be so immediately noticeable as well as the more obvious ones. There are some steps to discover these skills.

1. Take an objective look at what you do as a writer.

When you sit down to write something, take a moment and jot down all of the things that you're doing or are about to do. For example:

a. Create a story

b. Organize the idea

c. Create characters

d. Research/describe the setting of the story. Commit to a project from start to finish

2. Research the job descriptions of writers. Do a web search for "writer job description". This will give you some great insight into the skills built through writing.

a. Make a list of the skills you find in a few of the job descriptions.

b. Go through the list and pull out skills that you feel apply best to you and add them to the first list.

3. Research writers' websites and look at the services they provide. These services might give you some insight into skills you hadn't considered. Add them to your list.

4. Go to writing events and talk to other writers. There are conferences, festivals and networking events for a wide variety of topics. Find local writing events by doing a web search. Not only will you learn about the skills that you have developed, you might meet some cool new writing friends to support you in following your passion.

Flying Kites

Now we can move to a more fanciful hobby like flying kites. It may be tough to see that there are practical skills involved in this particular hobby but there are. For this example, we're going to assume that you also enjoy creating and building kites. Let's go through the same steps.

1. Take an objective look at what you do as a kite flyer.

a. Visualize the kite

b. Draw the vision

c. Figure out the materials you plan to use

d. Map out how you plan to put it together

e. Build the kite

f. Test the kite

g. Tweak the kite in case it doesn't fly properly the first time h. Commit to a project from start to finish

2. Research job descriptions of kite flyers and builders. You may not think these descriptions exist but you'd be surprised at the types of jobs that exist. Kite flying might very well be a viable job somewhere so it doesn't hurt to look.

3. Do some video website research. Find a how to video on kite making and make note of the steps. Then go through the steps objectively and pull out any skills you notice.

4. Research festivals, events and conferences related to kite building. Many of the more obscure or fanciful passions have festivals, events and parties created around them. These events will often have seminars and workshops that discuss the more technical aspects of the hobby. This is a great place to find those

hidden skills you may be developing by building and flying kites. As an added bonus, you will begin to meet people who share your passion and might make some new friends.

As you can see, it is very possible to find practical skills that are being developed by pursuing your passion. Plus since it's something you truly enjoy doing and actively pursue, you're going to be really good at it.

CHAPTER 2- WHAT IF YOU'VE LOST YOUR PASSION?

"Rest in reason; move in passion' – Khalil Gibran

Sometimes to unleash true passion in yourself, you may have to change your job to suit your aptitude better. But you may find that you do love your existing job, but simply don't feel very passionate about it. You can study your situation and then try to make a few changes to rekindle the passion you felt when you first started working.

Visualize yourself working passionately at your job. What would you be feeling? A sharp focus, clear vision of your future, total control and mastery over your work, a healthy body and an exuberant attitude! Then reverse engineer these symptoms to regain your passion.

Check on whether you work better with a team on the field rather than those solitary hours at a desk. Are you logical minded or creative minded? Are you crunching numbers when you would rather be in the design section? Get a revised aptitude assessment done. Ask your superior for a re-designation or transfer to a more appropriate department.

Exercise your body for at least thirty minutes every day. Let the adrenalin pump and flow in your blood. Eat healthy food and drink a lot of water. Quit smoking and using any stimulants. Restore the balance between your spirituality and physicality by meditation and prayer. Your refreshed body will invigorate your mind and passion will return.

Increase your knowledge of your field by taking new study courses. Take time out to travel and widen your perspective. Take a half-pay sabbatical to add new qualifications to your resume. Some lateral career movement can bring an innovative twist in your way of working.

Passion does not come overnight. Taking these proactive steps will see a gradual increase in your enthusiasm. You will begin working with a newly fired zeal which becomes contagious, motivating your team mates as well. You will have consciously taken charge of your life again and the fruits of prosperity will be in sight once again.

What drives passionate people to work so hard? Where do they get their energy from? Passion can be fueled by many factors. Let us examine 6 most important sources of the Force.

Using Curiosity to Re-Ignite Your Passion

One of the most powerful triggers of human invention has been curiosity. Why does something happen? How does lightning occur? What happens if you mix two chemicals? Which route will discover new lands? The human mind is programmed to question everything around it.

Discoveries take place when this curiosity becomes a passionate driving force. It takes on a relentless unstoppable energy which will not rest until a solution is found. Thomas Alva Edison tried out thousands of versions of the electric light bulb until he came up with one that worked. Madame Curie and her husband Pierre Curie spent all their lives unlocking the secrets of radioactivity. Steve Jobs' search for a better computer user interface finally gave us the Apple computer with the now familiar graphical user interface using icons, which eventually spread to the whole world of computing in the form of Microsoft's Windows.

Christopher Columbus, Vasco da Gama, Roald Amundsen and all the great explorers of the world travelled passionately in the quest of conquering new land for humanity. After centuries of looking up at the moon, Neil Armstrong and Edwin Aldrin actually walked on the lunar surface. Nothing can stop the force of curiosity and the determination that it fires up.

Success stories in the workplace often arise out of sheer ignorance. An employee may find he knows nothing about a particular field and begins learning it to satisfy his own curiosity. Pretty soon he has mastered it and is teaching the world a few new things about it. So step out of your 'known zone' and venture into the unknown. There just may be a discovery waiting there, with your name written on it.

Using Challenge to Revive Your Fire

Our search for the sources of passion brings us to yet powerful factor – Challenge.

A challenge can be posed by a person upon himself or by external forces. A personal challenge can arise from adverse circumstances of poverty or deprivation. Rags-to-riches stories have been told for hundreds of years now. Even Presidents of countries have arisen from humble beginnings and risen to their positions of power by the sheer force of their passion.

Family prestige and a desire to prove one's mettle to one's elders and t society can also act as a challenging force. When a son inherits a business built by his father, he is propelled to expand that enterprise and thus demonstrate his own prowess. While most companies have boards of directors and public equity, in many traditional societies, it is the family-driven businesses that persevere, even over the centuries.

Targets set by corporate leadership also act as challenged to work teams. A keen competitive spirit between rival groups can set off a passionate chase of the markets. Pepsi and Coca Cola, Nike and Adidas, are a couple of examples of passionate rivalry, with each seeking to outdo each other in the pursuit of a better product and more sales. In these mega rivalries, passionate employees move quickly up the corporate ladder. Belief in the company's goals and ideals is essential to engender passion in employees.

Sometimes the source of the challenge may lie closer to home. The love of a woman or one's children can drive a man to succeed with the intent of providing better care and education for them. We are motivated to buy a larger and better house, a bigger and faster car, the latest cell phones and clothes. All these must-haves also act as challenges and rewards for our work.

It is up to each individual to determine what challenges him or her and then as Nike's motto says – Just do it! Your natural challenge instinct will push you through. When a mountaineer was asked why he climbed a mountain, he answered – Because it is there! Its very existence as an insurmountable peak was a challenge to him!

I'm Living the Life I Want!
The Need to Leave a Legacy as a Passion-Driver

When you are young, your motivation for working and living lies in larger income, better standards of living and in general having a good time. But as you grow older, your priorities change. You want something more fulfilling. You seek to achieve goals that you will be remembered for. A sense of urgency begins to set in as time passes. And the source of your passion arises from wanting to leave behind a legacy.

That legacy may take the form of social change brought about by your work. Or it can be in an enterprise or institution founded by you. Many successful businessmen set up foundations and trusts in the pursuit of noble causes. Thus they seek to perpetuate their name or family name for posterity. An invention or a new process or a novel product can also enshrine the maker's name in the books of history.

Temporal pleasures and petty rewards do not satisfy someone working at this level. His or her passion seeks loftier goals and the greater the goal, the more fervent the passion. Revolutionaries and freedom fighters like Mahatma Gandhi and Che Guevara fought for the liberation of their countries. Their ambitions encompassed the lives of millions of their countrymen. The sheer magnitude of their legacy consumed their entire lifetime, but it was a passionate lifetime, with every day spent in pursuit of that goal.

How do you set about leaving behind your legacy? What is it that you feel strongly about? Write down your strongest emotions and issues. They may even lie outside your present work area. Start working on those issues. Educate yourself and acquire new skills if you have to, and get to work. It may be a simple project like improving your community, or a major reform of state laws. Remember that all the great men and women who have brought about change were ordinary men like you and me, but they had the power of conviction and passionate belief in their dreams.

Have Faith in Your Potential

One of the most powerful engines of passion is faith in an external agency. Though faith may seem to have been marginalized in today's seemingly rational society, it still works behind the scenes in many areas.

Religion plays a dominant role in the lives of millions of people in the world today. Priests, nuns, monks, sadhus and mullahs are known to accomplish tremendous feats of social work and penance. Their faith in God and their religious ideals is the rocket fuel in their lives.

The term evangelical fervor comes from a passion driven by a belief in God and the desire to convert other people to your way of thinking. This passion has sent explorers out to new lands, triggered numerous holy wars and changed entire demographics and cultures.

Oriental martial artists go through harsh training regimens and become lean mean human fighting machines. Their ruthless discipline arises from the strict codes of their specific martial art. Their devotion to this credo and their all-consuming faith in the mentor or sensei turns their lives into passionate experiences which are not for the feeble or faint of heart.

In modern sports we see the same phenomenon displayed with players and their coaches. A dynamic coach can inspire his team to put in a passionate performance. If the players do not have faith in the coach or their fellow team mates, the team fails to coordinate and the game is lost. The faith equation between sportsman and trainer is particularly important in endurance sports like gymnastics and athletics.

A footballer may in turn be driven by his faith in his fans. A corporate executive may be passionate about his employees and shareholders. Faith, emotion and inspiration are alive and kicking in every corner of human activity.

Which external agency are you focusing on? God? Your boss? Your coach? Your community or country? Decide on what moves you and use that agency as a star to guide you and drive your passion.

Passion for the Good of Mankind

Altruism is defined as 'unselfish regard for or devotion to the welfare of others' and also 'behavior by an animal that is not beneficial to or may be harmful to itself but that benefits others of its species'. How does altruism become a force of passion? In the ongoing recession we have seem millions of jobs being lost. Many of these people have taken up volunteer work in social or environmental organizations. And quite a number of them have discovered that this selfless work gives them more satisfaction than their high paying job ever gave them. Their paradigm has shifted from the prosperity of the body to the prosperity of the soul.

The concept of altruistic work has often been mocked by an aggressive materialistic society. Social workers are called 'do-gooders' and there is always a cynical and contemptuous ring to that phrase. But after years of ruthless ladder climbing, people often cherish the ability to be themselves and help other people. Bill Gates of Microsoft built a huge empire through ruthless corporate tactics, often getting embroiled in monopolistic practice lawsuits. But after all that, he set up an equally huge foundation that disburses vast sums of money to fight disease and improve education.

Altruism is generally overruled by stronger passions geared towards material success in the early years, but as age advances, altruistic thoughts resurface and become a primary passion in most of us. This is probably because we know that great people are remembered less for the millions that they make, but rather for their service to humanity.

No volunteer or social worker ever starved. While there aren't any millions to make in selfless service to the lesser privileged sections of humanity, the rewards of spiritual fulfillment are tremendous. The same passion that runs a corporate unit can be brought into play in running a successful Non-Governmental Organization or a Not for Profit outfit. All your skills can be well utilized in these noble ventures and you will see your passion suddenly multiply.

Can You Use Passion to Achieve Nirvana?

One of the definitions of epiphany is 'A comprehension or perception of reality by means of a sudden intuitive realization.' That's a moment in your life when you are suddenly struck by a powerful thought that changes your life forever.

A lifelong passion can be triggered by an epiphany. Saul the persecutor of the followers of Jesus Christ undergoes an epiphany on the road to Damascus and his life is changed forever. He went on to becoming one of Christ's greatest apostles.

Such a life changing incident occurs in the lives of many great men. It may be something provocative that someone says to you. It may be the sight of another human being suffering. It can be a sudden realization that you hate your present job and you decide what you really want to do in life. Sometimes an epiphany can be a harsh tragic event like the demise of a family member or some colossal disaster somewhere in the world. Your eyes open wide and all the shades fall off. You can see clearly around you and far ahead.

You do not have to sit and await an epiphany to change your life. Read good works of literature, listen to inspiring music and songs, travel around, meet people and you will be struck by a light on your own road to Damascus.

The Epiphany is also a Christian feast which celebrates God being revealed to Man in the form of Jesus Christ. So this can be taken as a metaphor for the spiritual being in us manifested in the physical form. Which is what passion is all about. Our spiritual energy driving our material body to achieve ideals and goals that are godlike! Inventors and discoverers experience epiphanies all the time. Archimedes was struck by his discovery of buoyancy and ran out yelling – Eureka! Eureka! May you too experience an epiphany and share old Archie's happiness!

CHAPTER 3- MONETIZING YOUR PASSION – YES, IT'S POSSIBLE!

Spend a moment to think about J. K. Rowling. Or think about Roger Ebert. Or think about Donald Trump. Or think about Paul Greengrass. These are people who are immensely rich. But what made them rich? They are rich not through things that they don't like to do – they are rich through the things they really like to do, things that they think they exist for.

J. K. Rowling had a passion for writing ever since she could remember. She began writing when she was a kid. Despite the various difficulties in her life, she did not give up. She continued writing whenever she could. With two kids in tow, this woman conjured the biggest fiction phenomenon of our generation – Harry Potter. When she made Harry Potter, did she think she would become richer than the Queen? Not at all. She just wrote it out. She gave vent to her passion. The rest just happened.

I'm Living the Life I Want!

There's probably no cinematophile as crazy for movies as Roger Ebert is. He writes reviews for practically every movie that's released. See how he has converted his passion for movies into his work? His movie reviews are the most highly-prized and he gets paid handsomely for watching movies and penning his keen observation about them!

Need one say anything about Donald Trump? Business is his forte, his passion. And he is unstoppable there. When he has one venture running, he invests into another. He doesn't even have the time to stop and think about the money. He is just giving vent to his innate passion, allowing it to manifest itself in whatever way it can.

Paul Greengrass is known as one of the most upstart directors in Hollywood today. His directorial styles have been criticized earlier, especially his penchant for using shaky camera moves, but did he bend his style to please his early detractors? No, he didn't! And what did he come up with? The Bourne series, that's what! And his movies have become cult. Not to forget, he's become quite filthy rich.

These are just some of the famous people who made it big by doing what they love to do.

As for you, once you've identified the practical skills behind your passion pursuit, you can consider having it make money for you. The really cool thing about any kind of specialized interest is that there are other people out there who share that interest. When your interest is really unique, it can be a very niche market but those people are also often very involved in their unique interests. But even if your passion is in a more general arena, there are ways to make money from it.

Find a Job

Since you've already done some research on job descriptions that relate to your passion, you can look further into those descriptions to see the kinds of companies that hire those people. If you are able to secure a job and use your career to pursue your passion, kudos! Many people aren't able to work in an area they're passionate about and you should fully enjoy and appreciate this opportunity. If you don't find a job right away, consider volunteering for an organization. You could support a positive cause while doing something you love.

Start a Membership Website/List

Many experts create websites or email lists where they share information on a regular basis for a monthly fee. If you enjoy flying and building kites, you could consider creating a membership list where you email members weekly tips on how to build better kites. Membership programs are great because they create income that comes in on a regular basis. As long as you continue to provide valuable information and good service to the members of your list, you'll have a steady stream of income. One way to get subscribers for your list is by attending those events, festivals and conferences mentioned in the previous chapter. You can request people's email addresses and find out if they'd be interested in signing up.

Create a Blog

Blogging is very popular and can be a great way to share your knowledge and passion while making money from it. With a blog you can make money promoting products, selling ad space or selling products. Plus, by blogging about something, you get the opportunity to showcase your knowledge and discuss your passion.

Chapter 4- Professional Photography Made More Profitable Online

You would have to live in a shack out in the woods like the Unabomber to not be exposed to literally hundreds of photographs per day. Think about your daily life. If you ate breakfast this morning, there was probably a picture of someone on the cereal box. If you made coffee, there might be a picture on the can, and that's just in your kitchen.

There are photos on the billboards as you drive to work. There are photos in the magazines when you sit in your dentist's waiting room, and you are bombarded with photos galore the moment you turn on your computer and start browsing the Internet.

The point is every industry needs photographs. And while there are many experts out there who get paid very handsomely for the photographs they churn out (think major magazine photographers), amateurs are able to make great money doing what they love, too!

That's right. You don't have to be a professional. You can go out right now, pick up a digital camera and you can theoretically start making money off of those photographs. And I'm going to show you how.

First, however, before you rush out thinking you're the next Annie Leibovitz, you need to consider if you have what it takes to make money from your photos.

That can be a hard thing to ascertain, especially when you have a passion for something. Because the truth is, you could enthusiastically take loads and loads of pictures but there's no guarantee that any of them will sell.

To fail at something you love to do can hurt deep down in your core. But you must remember that just because your photo doesn't sell, doesn't mean you're no good. It could be for a number of reasons.

The point is to have patience, and make sure you learn how it's done before you start selling your photos for money.

Requirements to Successfully Sell Photos Online

If you think it's easy to sell digital photos online, you're mistaken. Show me one person who's made it big selling photos, and I'll show you ten more just like him/her that don't make squat. They could even be taking pictures of the same things. The difference between them is that the person who made it put time and effort into his/her photo business. So ask yourself, do you have what it takes to sell your digital photos online?

I'm Living the Life I Want!

If you said yes, then you must commit yourself if you hope to make it.

Go back and read that sentence again. That's the most important aspect of making money through digital photography. You must put in the required time and you must remain passionate about what you're doing because that passion, or lack of it, will come out in your photos. And finally, you must be able to have patience until you've learned enough to actually know which photos will sell, and which ones won't.

Time

The amount of money you make with your photos depends on how much time you invest in your business. On average, you should expect to work at least four hours per week, and more if you're really ambitious. Four hours is nothing and it's worth it when you consider you're doing what you love.

Are You Creative?

This is a huge one. You can take a thousand pictures of your cat and it's likely not one of them will sell for even a penny. That's because cats have been done. You need to step out of your immediate surroundings, get out of your comfort zone, and you need to think outside the box.

Carry your camera with you wherever you go and be on the lookout for an image that just screams, "Take my picture!" This could be a shard of ice hanging from a lighthouse bridge. It could be a neighborhood dog catching a Frisbee, or it could be the way the sunset splashes vivid colors across the darkened sky.

Equipment

Obviously, if you're going to sell digital photos, you're going to need a digital camera. But to increase your chances of making a sale, you might want to invest in a few other things, as well.

The camera is number one. You must have a digital camera. There are many on the market these days and most of them produce excellent quality photographs. The prices are dropping on them all the time, so you should be able to get a decent one for cheap.

But what about editing software? Have you considered that you may want to doctor your photos so that they come out absolutely perfect? Do you know how to use that editing software to its fullest potential? Finally, do you even know how to take good photos?

These are all questions you really need to consider before you try your hand at this lucrative but competitive business.

There is a lot of money to be made, but there's also beautiful photography to be made, as well. It really is a great way to earn a living. It's fun, and there's just something fulfilling knowing that others are willing to pay for the photos you've taken. However, you must also be ready to deal with rejection - because that can be the most difficult part of this whole business.

Rejection

You may find that you're in love with your photos, but that you're the only one who feels that way. It's kind of like when someone brings along their dog and they go on and on about how cute and loveable their dog is, but everyone else doesn't feel that way. Some people may be allergic to dogs. The dog may be lovable but

I'm Living the Life I Want!

that doesn't mean they want to risk touching it so they'll blow up like a balloon.

The point is you can't please everybody. If you take a beautiful photograph and nobody likes it, don't let it get you down. Those people just don't have good taste, that's all. Or they don't need that photograph for any particular reason.

See, most people buy photos because they're looking for a particular one. They may need a butterfly photo for a website, or a doctor photo for a brochure. Part of this business is making sure your photos get seen by the right people, but we'll get into that later.

You must be able to deal with rejection or else you'll never make it in the photography business. If you don't make any sales, just keep doing what you're doing and give it time. You must have patience until your efforts begin to pay off.

Work day by day, little by little, and before you know it you'll know what it takes to sell photos online and you'll have done it from pure knowledge and hard work.

How to Choose the Right Camera

If you don't already have a camera, you know you need one. But you're likely going to find a lot of choices out there. There are so many different types of cameras, brands and accessories that it can seem almost overwhelming. However, picking out a good camera isn't that difficult at all.

Simply get online and start researching the cameras you come across based on a few criteria. You'll want to be focused on the amount of megapixels the camera has, as well as the quality of the sensor. But of course price is going to be an issue, as well. So your job is to find a camera that offers the most for the least amount of money. That sounds obvious, but it's not easy when you're bombarded by so many different types of digital cameras.

However, there are a couple ways you can go about getting a camera that's of good enough quality to take excellent photographs.

Experts

If you want to know something about a subject, you turn to an expert, right? In keeping with that same thinking, camera experts are who you should turn to when you're trying to find the perfect camera for you.

You can find experts online on consumer report websites, or you can read reviews by experts that are posted online. You can also ask clerks that work in the camera sections of your favorite stores. These employees spend all day looking at, talking about, and learning about digital cameras. Ask them plenty of questions and tell them what you're trying to do.

You will want to make sure that the camera you choose is at least a 5 megapixel camera. Remember that just because the megapixel count is high, doesn't mean the photos are going to be better. Make sure the sensor is of high quality, as well.

Most people find that cameras where you are able to change the lenses produce better quality images, but you should be fine with your everyday run-of-the-mill digital camera.

I'm Living the Life I Want!
Digital Photo Editing

If you don't know how to properly edit a photograph, you're starting out with a huge disadvantage. You may think that digital editing is cheating. After all, the photo should be sold based on the natural beauty of the image captured. There should be no editing going on. If it's not in the photo, then you shouldn't be paid for it.

There are a lot of old timers stuck in their ways that still hold onto that idea. But the fact is every industry uses digital editing to enhance photography.

Programs like Photoshop and other digital editing software allow you to do all sorts of things to enhance a photograph in order to prime it for sale. Not only can you take the red out of someone's eyes, but you can crop, change colors, change an object's density, create shadow detail, and that's just to name a few.

So if you don't know how to use any of the common programs out there for editing the photographs you take, it's recommended that you get one so that you can stay abreast or ahead of the competition who will surely be using it.

Getting Your Money from Microstock Photography

You may have heard of stock photography. This is where an image is licensed to be used by a specific person for a specific reason. For instance, a webmaster may need a certain type of photo for a website. Instead of risking taking one off the Internet and getting into copyright issues once the site becomes successful; the webmaster decides to buy the image so that he can use it legally.

Stock agencies are typically very picky about who they accept as photographers. So if you don't have that much experience, but you're still excited with the concept of making money with your photos, you'll be happy to know that an offshoot of stock photography exists on the Internet. This is known as Microstock photography.

Microstock photography sites encourage professionals, amateurs and hobbyists alike to submit their photos for sale. These sites get almost all of their photos from individuals just like you, and they're also known for their low prices. That's both good and bad news for you.

The good news is that the low prices mean that customers are likely to keep coming back for more. You could form a long relationship with a client who loves your work and can only afford to pay the nominal fee the site charges for your photos. Now, consider if the same client had to pay hundreds of dollars for a photo. You may not see that client again after that, unless your reputation preceded you.

These Microstock sites typically charge anywhere from $.20 to $10.00. While that may not seem like much money, it adds up if you're a good enough photographers and you're able to sell a lot of photos.

Selling your photos on these sites sounds great, doesn't it? All you have to do is take the photo and the site does the selling for you. Believe me; this is much better than taking your photos and trying to sell them yourself. While you can make more money doing your own marketing and selling, you're likely going to put in a whole lot more time than you make in dollars. It would be best to use one of these sites until you're good enough to venture out on your own.

Now, let's take a look at some of these Microstock photography sites so that you can decide which one(s) to use.

I'm Living the Life I Want!
Where to Sell Your Photos

Now that you have a camera and you're ready to publish them online so that you can make some money, it's time to find some Microstock sites to add your photos to.

You'll find that some sites pay more than others, and you'll also find a variation in the pay terms as well as methods of payment. Hopefully, this guide will help you choose one that's right for your needs.

Shutterstock

This Microstock site can be extremely lucrative, but first you have to be accepted. The main complaint you may hear about Shutterstock is that they're picky about who they accept for their site. To get accepted, you must send in ten photos and have at least seven of them accepted by a review team.

It's important to understand how stock photography works, and you also must have good equipment. It's not uncommon to have to try a few times before getting accepted on this site. But if you can get in, the income potential is quite high.

Dreamstime

This Microstock site has a proven track record and it gets many visitors per day, as well as many sales. When you submit your photos to Dreamstime, you stand to make 50% commission on each sale you make. The best part is that you don't have to send any test photos in order to get accepted. So this might be a good site to start with until you get a little more experience.

It must be stated that even though they accept unknown photographers, they do check all of the images they receive and they will reject any photos that they deem are of a lower quality.

Fotolia

Fotolia is sort of new on the Microstock scene. They are quickly gaining popularity, however, and they have customers that span the globe. Fotolia isn't known for its high commissions but your prices can go up once you gain through the ranks and get more sales.

The single most heard complaint about Fotolia, besides their long upload time, is the fact that they have a blacklist which includes all photos they no longer need. If you shoot a lot of horse photos, for instance, you may find that the site is saturated with them and that horses are now on that list.

Shutterstock, Dreamstime and Fotolia are the main microstock sites that most people use to successfully sell their photos. However, new sites are popping up all the time.

When choosing a site, make sure you're dealing with a legitimate site. Whenever something becomes popular on the Internet, such as making money by taking digital photos, it seems that crooks and scam artists can't wait to capitalize on poor, unwitting individuals who just want to make a few bucks using their passion and talent.

So check out all the sites you're considering before you register. Check user reviews, really look at the site's operations and make sure you will be paid when your photos do indeed sell.

CHAPTER 5- CRAFTING OTHER PRODUCTS FROM YOUR PASSION

As I mentioned in the last chapter, selling products is a great way to monetize a blog but you can create and sell your own products without having a blog. Ideally, you should have some access to an interested audience of people to buy your products but even if you don't, you can still benefit by creating some. Now that you've done some research into your topic of interest and you know that you're not alone, you can rest assured that there are customers for your products.

Ebook

Ebooks are a great way to share your knowledge about a topic easily and independently. Typically, eBooks aren't expected to be hundreds of pages long which make them much easier to write than a novel. The length isn't as important as the quality of information but it should be more than just a few pages to make sure the buyers of it feel they've gotten their money's worth. As you know, many people purchase and read eBooks (like you're doing right now!) on their computers, smart phones or tablets on a regular basis. The key is to ensure that the information being provided is valuable. Even if you're writing on a topic that you're very knowledgeable about, do some research to make the book the best it can be.

Video Course

If you prefer talking to writing, a video course is another way to monetize your passion. All you need is a camera that can shoot video, a tripod and an easy video editing program. Most computers (both MAC and PC) come with a basic video editing program. MACs come with iMovie and PCs come with Windows Movie Maker. However if your computer doesn't have either, you can download Adobe Premiere Elements, which is another easy to use video editing program that works on both operating systems. You can download a trial to practice using it with limitations and then upgrade for less than $100. Once you have the technical tools, you're ready to record but now you need a plan for your course.

1. Determine the goal of your course or your desired outcome. It helps to know the end result of the course then you can work backwards.

2. Write out the steps required to meet your desired outcome. Make sure you write it in the correct order as if you're going to tell someone how to do it in writing.

3. Decide how many videos you want in the course. Try to keep the course nice and tight but don't cram too much in one video. Ideally, an online video should be no more than 8 minutes long.

4. Create a plan for what you will cover in each video. Don't write a script. You will be tempted to memorize it and won't sound natural

in your videos. Give yourself an outline to make sure you touch on all of the steps.

Now that you have everything you need, it's time to record your videos. Make sure you do it in a quiet room with good lighting. Be clear but concise in your instructions. Practice a little if necessary. It might be odd to see yourself on camera if this is your first time so do some test runs to get used to it.

Webinar Course

If you don't have a video camera or don't want to be on camera, you can do a webinar course that doesn't require that you be on camera in person. You will need to provide your voice and expertise, but that's it. The steps to creating a webinar course are similar to creating a video course.

1. Determine the goal of your course or your desired outcome.

2. Write out the steps required to meet your desired outcome. Make sure you write it in the correct order as if you're going to tell someone how to do it in writing.

3. Decide how many modules you want in the course. Try to keep it nice and tight and don't cram too much information into one module.

4. Create a presentation in PowerPoint or a similar program. This will be your plan but also provide visual materials for the people who will be participating in your webinar. If they can't see your lovely face, they should have a cool presentation to see.

Once you have these pieces organized, use a program like Web Ex which can cost up to $89 per month or anymeeting.com which can cost up to $69.99 per month. Both have free options which have limitations but may work when you're just starting out. If you're unsure how your products should look, do a web search for others that are similar to what you'd like to create. The web is a great repository of products that have been created and can be used to provide an example that you can work from.

Ideally, you would have a website or blog that you could use to market your products, but that isn't necessary. There are online marketplaces like Clickbank and Paydotcom where individuals can sell information products that they create. There are pros and cons to all marketplaces so do your research and make sure you read the fine print, carefully. Many people don't pay much attention to the terms listed on most websites but if you're selling your products, it's important that you do. You want to make sure that you understand and truly agree to those terms before you click to create an account and start selling your products

CHAPTER 6- AN ETHICAL APPROACH TO MONETIZING YOUR PASSION

It is quite possible to make money out of your passion, but as it is with any other moneymaking opportunity, you must remember that there are some principles and ethics that you need to follow. We shall take a look at some of them here.

1. It is highly important that you respect whatever it is that you are dealing with. If your passion is coin collecting, make sure you bring about the right reverence to your activities. You cannot start blatantly criticizing and abusing this subject. Well, you could criticize, but then you have to justify what you say. Remember that you are trying to make money here. Since your target audience is going to be other people who are also passionate about this

subject, you will not earn anything if you sling mud at it without reason.

2. Be knowledgeable. People who will come to you already know the basics. What they want to learn is the viewpoint of another expert in the subject. Make absolutely certain that you know all the terms well and that your facts are right.

3. Keep up with the times. Things are going to change fast, whatever your scope of interest is. Always keep on the move learning new things. It could be a great idea to use Google Alerts which can tell you what's happening around you.

4. Be responsive. When people reach out to you, they are hoping to commingle with someone else who has the same likes as them. They are reaching out with some expectations in their mind. Don't belie these. If you do, you are effectively stopping other people from reaching out to you as well.

This brings us to the fifth principle: Always network with people. If you are trying to make money out of a subject that you are very passionate about, network with other likeminded people. The more people you network with, the more will you be talked about.

Making Money without Forgetting Passion at Home

Getting passionate about your career and blazing a glorious path at the office is great. But don't let your loved ones suffer from a lack of passion at home. A proper balance has to be struck by giving love to your spouse and children too.

A passionate lifelong affair with your wife or husband can do wonders in your work life too. You are happy and relaxed and your body glows with the healing effects of healthy loving sex. The love you shower on your children is also reciprocated many times over.

A man is truly respected if he excels in all his roles – as a worker, a son, a husband and a father (and even a grandfather) and a community member. Devote time and passion to all these roles. When you have genuinely mastered the art of passion, you will find that it pervades every minute of your day, be it in the boardroom or bedroom or playroom.

Passion can become a double-edged sword if not wielded properly. Spending hours and hours of obsessed extra time at the workplace can affect your health as well as your family relations. Neglecting to attend your son's school events and not cheering him at his football match can create an alienation that can never be repaired. An unfulfilled spouse can also prove very damaging in the long run. A marriage can fall apart and a string of unhappy one night stands can never take the place of a loving caring relationship.

Passion is not about throwing huge family parties where everyone can feed on your wealth. It isn't about giving a no-limit credit card to your wife or the latest bike to your son. It is spending time and effort to share your life and soul with your loved ones. Passion lies in transmitting your passion for life to your children, your wife and all around you.

Chapter 7- Secret Strategies to Passion Income – Unveiled!

So, how do you plan a strategy to monetarily tap into your passion? There are some qualities that they must possess.

Their Potential

It is necessary that the strategies have a good potential. When we speak about potential in the context of the Internet, we mean that they should be able to reach out to your niche. So, if you are considering article marketing or blogging, you have to do it in such a way that it reaches it to people who might be interested in what you have to say. You might not want to use a method such as affiliate marketing, for instance, because you might feel this method won't reach out to your niche.

Another thing that you need to think about is that you should be comfortable using this particular method. You should have the technical knowledge to use this strategy. There are ways in which you can hire people to accomplish tasks for you, such as you could hire someone to set up a blog for you or someone to write content for you, but it is important that you have the overall knowhow about the strategy that you are using.

The Expense

All right, we are trying to make money out of something you are passionate about. The keyword here is that you are trying to 'make money'. So, should you invest a lot at the start? On the Internet, you are likely to find ways that can help you promote your substance for free as well as for a lot of money. The efficacy of these methods will be different. But, you need to do your research and find out a method that doesn't cost much, but reaches out to your target population.

Plan out your strategies for the long term. You don't need to use a method that will not pay you out tomorrow. At the same time, plan out a strategy that won't impose a lot on your time. There are several methods that you can use spending only a few minutes of your day, which we shall be seeing shortly.

You Lose Nothing if You Live Your Passion with Intention

Once you've identified your passion and found some practical uses for it, the hard part comes next. Living your passion won't be easy. You may find yourself having to defend it to family and friends.

While standing up for your passion may be a challenge, it won't be the hardest one. You will have to consistently work with yourself to stay true to doing what you love. If you've made it all the way to adulthood without pursuing your passion, there's sometimes a very compelling reason; fear. It's not easy to put yourself out there to potentially be judged, especially if your passion is considered impractical. It can also be scary to do something that you aren't familiar with or comfortable doing. This fear is natural and shouldn't be used as an excuse not to move forward. If you have found something that you enjoy, it's worth it to pursue it.

Another thing that prevents more people from following their passion is failure. The fear of failure is one of the strongest and most paralyzing ones. However, the fear of success may be just as strong. Sometimes it's easier to simply sit and dream about what could be than it is to actually go out and do it. Both success and failure carry with them their own level of responsibility but in either case, you've made the first step and tried. We can often be our own worst critics, especially when it comes to stepping outside of our own box and doing something different.

Negative and doubtful self-talk is natural but it shouldn't stop you. Neither should you not knowing what to do next. Yes, I've given you some steps to follow but if you noticed, many of them involved doing some research. We live in a society where information is an important commodity and it's very readily available. Take advantage of it. Just as not following your passion brings with it the responsibility of a dream unfulfilled, following your passion and being successful brings with it the responsibility that comes with that success.

The great thing about following through with something that's risky is that even if you do fail, you can rest comfortably knowing that you tried. If you do nothing at all, you never know what could have

I'm Living the Life I Want!
been. Happiness is a decision. If you make the decision that you are going to follow your passion and that it will make you happy, it will.

ABOUT THE AUTHOR

Ruth Thompson is a professional photographer and blogger. She used to write at the local newspaper and was a freelance photographer in downtown Detroit. Her life and career changed when she realized the potential of monetizing her passion and selling online.

Today, Ruth is a frequent guest at seminars and conferences, where she shares how she has successfully made thousands per month selling what she loves to do.